Research on the EDGE

RAIN FORESTS

LOUISE SPILSBURY

A+

Smart Apple Media

Published by Smart Apple Media, an imprint of Black Rabbit Books

P.O. Box 3263, Mankato, Minnesota 56002

www.smartapplemedia.com

Published by arrangement with Wayland Books, London.

Cataloging-in-Publication Data is available from the Library of Congress

ISBN: 978-1-62588-156-4   (library binding)

ISBN: 978-1-62588-576-0   (eBook)

Picture acknowledgments

Cover: Corbis: Pete Oxford/Minden Pictures main; Shutterstock: Christopher Meder top; Inside: Dreamstime: Adifor 11b, Nateskate66 18b, Paura 11t, Spphotos 18t, 24b; Forest Stewardship Council: 26t; Getty Images: Tengku Bahar/AFP 9, Timothy G. Laman/National Geographic 8; Istockphoto: Guenterguni 17; Shutterstock: 7, Silvano Audisio 23b, Stephane Bidouze 1, 23t, Dirk Ercken 20b, Frontpage 29, Gopause 22, Ben Heys 19, Kjersti Joergensen 28b, Dmitry Kalinovsky 25, NH 5t, Boivin Nicolas 28t, Orange Line Media 21, Vadim Petrakov 20t, Scott Prokop 26b, Alexander Raths 27, Dr. Morley Read 10, 13t, Lisette van der Hoorn 6, Kirsanov Valeriy Vladimirovich 16b, Worldswildlifewonders 13b, Adam Ziaja 24t, Egon Zitter 5t; Wikimedia Commons: Nireekshit 12, Vaikoovery 14–15.

Printed in the United States by CG Book Printers

North Mankato, Minnesota

PO 1724

2-2015

CONTENTS

WORKING IN A RAIN FOREST

Hot, steamy, rainy, overgrown, muddy, thorny, full of biting insects and other animals that can cause harm. Rain forests are extreme environments, yet some scientists work there every day, researching plants, animals, soils, and other aspects of these wild, remote places.

A Study in Biodiversity

Rain forests are natural laboratories with incredible *biodiversity*, from enormous trees to tiny orchids and millions of different animals living in, on, or among the plants. Scientists study in rain forests to learn more about the remarkable *organisms* that live there and how they interact. They also hope to discover new *species*, partly because these discoveries may help scientists develop new medicines and materials.

Scientists research tropical rain forests to try to improve our understanding of the unique plants and animals in this amazing *ecosystem*.

DANGER!

Tens of millions of species of insects live in rain forests. Some are just irritating but others can harm researchers. For example, tiny sweat bees crowd onto any uncovered flesh to lick salt from sweat, while bot flies lay their eggs under human skin. Stings from wild rain forest bees and bullet ants are extremely painful.

What Scientists Study

Scientists also find out how the changes to forests that are caused by people, such as *deforestation*, affect the *climate* and the forest water supply. Working with foreign governments and local people, scientists use their findings to conserve rain forests worldwide. In this book, we will look at how the scientists carry out their research, what they do with their results, and some of the discoveries they have made.

Colourful pitcher plants grow on the mossy branches of rain forest trees.

> Rhinoceros beetles look fearsome but they are harmless to people. The male's large horns are used to fight other males in the rain forest.

RAIN FOREST LIFE

Thousands of scientists work in rain forests every year, each with a different research focus. They come to the rain forest because of the immense biodiversity and because rain forests, and the organisms within them, are disappearing.

▼ Rain forest trees are mostly hardwoods that are valuable but can be slow-growing. Once logged, the rain forest does not regrow quickly and some tree species die out.

Rain Forests under Pressure

Some researchers study threats to rain forest wildlife. For example, while rain forest animals are under threat from hunters who kill them for meat, hunting affects plants in the forest, too. In 2010, researchers proved that the *poaching* of elephants was linked to a loss of trees such as the star apple. This is because after eating the fruit, the elephants spread the seeds of these trees through their *droppings*.

Jaguars are hunted for their beautiful coats, but are also disappearing as people kill the animals jaguars hunt for food.

Rain Forest Discovery

Scientists also study tropical rain forests to find new species. Rain forests are home to half of the world's estimated 10 million plant and animal species. So far, scientists think they have discovered only about 6 percent of these, and they are finding new things all the time. In 2008, researchers using Google Earth even spotted a completely new area of rain forest on Mount Mabu in Mozambique that had never before been charted!

DANGER!

Scientists in the field have to look out for forest elephants, particularly in some African rain forests, where elephant attacks are increasing. Elephants are not naturally aggressive, but because forests are shrinking, they are more likely to meet and be scared by people, such as farmers protecting their fields.

RAIN FOREST GEAR

Scientists working in the rain forest use a variety of equipment, depending on their field of research.

Traps to Thermometers

Scientists studying wildlife need to collect or view animals to study. To do this, they may use pooters, which are tubes that suck up and collect insects and other small animals. Light traps are lit-up sheets that attract insects, such as moths, at night. Camera traps automatically take a photograph of any animal that breaks an *infrared* light beam. Scientists studying the weather use thermometers, rainfall gauges, and *humidity* and gas *sensors*. They determine locations using *GPS* devices. Most scientists record data and observations using notebooks and pens, laptops, cameras, and sound recorders.

▼ Moths are attracted to light, so researchers set up simple light traps like this one. A light is suspended in front of a white sheet and the moths fly onto the sheet where they can be examined.

Facing Challenges

The rain forest climate can damage some equipment or make it tricky to use. For example, *water vapor* from the high humidity can easily fog camera lenses. Water, dust, or small ants get into laptops, cameras, and mobile phones, causing the machines to overheat, or electronic damage that stops the devices from working. Even the labs are under threat as wooden buildings can be eaten away by invading termites!

▼ This tapir has been fitted with a radio transmitter collar that scientists can use to track its movements in the Malaysian rain forest where it lives.

CUTTING EDGE

Keeping sight of animals is tricky in dense rain forests, so scientists use wireless telemetry. They attach or surgically implant light radio transmitters in animals and then use hand-held aerials and radios to track the direction and strength of the signal from the transmitters. Computers are used to record and analyze movement *data* and display results.

ROUGH AND REMOTE

The quickest, easiest way for researchers to reach their isolated rain forest research labs is usually by boat. In rain forest regions with few rivers or no major roads, scientists often take a helicopter from the nearest city to their research site.

Walk to Work

After they have been dropped off, scientists may be able to travel the rest of the journey by road or they may have to walk to their research station. Walking causes the least damage or disruption to remote habitats. However, walking through the rain forest is slow progress, partly because fast-growing vines and branches clog up trails. Researchers often have to hack their way through tough forest undergrowth with sharp machetes.

Rain forest like this area surrounding the Amazon River is so thick that trails can easily become overgrown.

CUTTING EDGE

Remote labs have poor or nonexistent mobile phone and landline coverage, so scientists keep in touch with others using *satellite* phones. These transmit and receive voice and data signals to and from satellites orbiting Earth. The phones are small and cheap so even scientists working with low research budgets can use them.

Scientists use kayaks and inflatable boats to travel and bring equipment and supplies to remote rain forest settlements where ferry services are infrequent.

Four-by-fours must carry fuel supplies and tools to fix vehicles—there are few garages in the rain forest!

Road Problems

Many of the roads researchers have to travel on in rain forests are rough, winding mud tracks. Some are pitted with deep, wide holes, which damage vehicles that drive into them. Rain storms often wash away stretches of road completely. Scientists usually use 4x4s and other vehicles with knobby tires to grip rough roads. Some vehicles even have aerial exhaust pipes so they do not suck up muddy water when traveling through puddles.

RESPECTING THE FOREST

When scientists live and work in the rain forest they have to take care not to damage the very things—plants, wildlife, and environment—they have come to research.

Reducing Impacts

To avoid cutting down trees for fuel, scientists cook on kerosene stoves or solar cookers, which use shiny surfaces to intensify heat from sunlight onto a cooking pot. They carefully remove

Lab buildings can be made from local timber. Fences to keep out wild animals are made of smooth wire that will not injure wildlife.

garbage, such as plastic bags or cans, which can trap and harm rain forest animals. For building, they try to use local materials that are *renewable* or in high supply rather than bringing in truckloads of materials made elsewhere, which would cause *pollution* and the need to build more roads.

Protecting the Canopy

More than two-thirds of all organisms in the rain forest live in the *canopy*, the highest parts of the trees that can be 100 feet (30 m) above the ground. In the past, scientists studied canopy life by cutting down trees or spraying chemicals to kill or stun animals so they dropped to the ground. Today, they use gentler techniques. Mountaineering equipment allows scientists to reach high branches safely. Researchers also construct canopy walkways, observation towers, and platforms.

Fixed bridges let scientists move between rain forest trees without any risk of damaging branches and the plants and animals that live and grow on them.

CUTTING EDGE

In 2012, architect Yi Yvonne Weng designed a Canopy Trail. This is a light mesh of carbon fiber and metal rods like a spider's web that can be spread over the canopy. Scientists can use tear-drop-shaped pods suspended from the mesh as mobile labs between the trees.

RAIN FOREST LAB

Scientists working in rain forests need buildings in which to live, plan, and discuss their research, and store and study their samples and collected data. They do this in research stations or labs.

Different Shapes and Sizes

There is a huge range of rain forest labs. Some are just tents or tarps stretched over branches. Others are large buildings with well-equipped labs, classrooms, dining areas, and bedrooms. Most labs are in remote places, so staff set up systems to clean water for drinking, dispose of waste, and generate electricity by *photovoltaic* (PV) panels, which use the abundant sunlight of a rain forest.

Agumbe, India

Agumbe Rainforest Research Station (ARRS) in southwest India is a typical rain forest lab. Its facilities include a laboratory where researchers study local wildlife such as king cobras, and a small library and reading room. There is also an office for the director of ARRS.

The living areas of Agumbe include dormitories with bunk beds for visiting scientists and *conservation* volunteers, a lounge with chairs and tables, and a basic kitchen with a cooker, sink, and preparation area. There is no fridge because the power supply is variable.

Surrounding the main building are a toilet and shower block with solar-heated water, cottages for resident staff, and a garden in which food is grown. The station has a 4x4 and motorbikes to pick up visitors, fetch supplies, and for emergencies—the nearest hospital is more than 18.6 miles (30 km) away.

Agumbe Rainforest Research Station is a simple building with a watertight roof to keep out heavy rain forest rainfall.

CUTTING EDGE

Daintree Research Station in Australia has a 154-foot (47-m) crane with a long arm and platform at the top. The crane can rotate 360 degrees so that scientists can study an area of the upper rain forest measuring 2.47 acres (1 hectare).

Scientists observe and track forest wildlife from the crane platform at Daintree Research Station.

LIFE IN THE LAB

Scientists working in the rain forest need to dress appropriately for the conditions. Many wear long-sleeved shirts and trousers to protect their skin from sunburn and scratches or rashes caused by thorny, poisonous plants and biting insects. Sunscreen and insect repellents are also essential. Scientists wear comfortable boots to prevent blisters because in humid, dirty rain forest conditions, a small blister can become a painful wound if it is infected.

After a day of observation and data collection, scientists gather to eat a meal before further scientific study in the evening.

Using a head lamp at night allows scientists to attract and study nocturnal animals, but they may also attract stinging or irritating insects.

On the Lookout

In the rain forest people need to constantly be aware of dangers. For example, they check their boots before putting them on in case a scorpion or venomous centipede has crawled inside. They also always check with locals before venturing into a rain forest river. There is always the danger that stingrays, piranhas, or *caimans* are in the water!

 Scientists may patiently observe worms in the wild for long periods until they gather enough data to reveal patterns of behavior.

Scientific Research

It can be fascinating and thrilling to study rain forests, but it is also usually time-consuming. Rain forest scientists rarely have a day off. Locating organisms to study within a rain forest can take many days, and evenings may be spent writing notes, studying in the library, and examining samples collected during the day.

DANGER!

Fungi grow on any warm, damp surface, from clothing and food to people's feet. Foot rot is a fungal infection that happens when feet are never properly dry. In the rain forest, scientists have to wash their feet and socks daily. They also dry their feet carefully and apply ointment or powder to keep foot rot at bay.

PEOPLE OF THE RAIN FOREST

There are around 50 million tribal people living in the world's rain forests, most of them in the vast Amazon rain forest of South America. Researchers can learn much from working with these people. Many survive in part on forest resources such as wood and wild honey.

> Long ago, South American tribes discovered that some rain forest trees produce milky latex when their bark is cut. Today people use latex to make products such as rubber and chewing gum.

Knowledge Base

Rain forest tribes, especially their healers, have expert knowledge of forest plants and animals that is passed down through generations. A single Amazonian tribe, such as the Yanomani, may use more than 200 different plants as medicines. Many of the medicines we use today, such as aspirin, were discovered when scientists studied how rain forest tribes use plants.

This rain forest guide is using a leaf to drink fresh water naturally stored within a tree trunk.

Local Skills

Researchers also rely on local people in other ways. For example, they may buy food, mosquito nets, and insect repellent from local businesses. They employ local people as cooks or expert animal trackers. Scientists setting up canopy walkways or research centers may also help to establish tourism businesses run by local people, who act as guides and give talks to visitors about their land and cultures. Scientists often rely on tribal people to help them locate new species, and to learn more about known ones.

▼ Tribal people use their detailed knowledge of the routes and organisms of the rain forest to lead groups of visitors.

DANGER!

Locals know which rain forest plants to avoid. For example, the stinging tree has fine, poisonous hairs on its leaves that can give people painful rashes for two months. The finger cherry can cause blindness if eaten, and raw cashew nuts are highly poisonous.

RICHES OF THE RAIN FOREST

Each year, research scientists find about 2,000 new rain forest species and discover more about existing rain forest organisms, too.

New Species

Most discoveries are of small animals, such as new beetles and spiders, but large animals are found, too. New species of giant rat, monkey, parrot, dolphin, and anaconda were just a few of the 1,200 species discovered in the Amazon rain forest between 1999 and 2009.

 The Amazon anaconda that was discovered in 2009 was the first anaconda species found worldwide since 1936. It can grow to 13 feet (4 m) long and it hunts caimans and jaguars.

Some drugs are derived from the poisonous skin of certain rain forest treefrogs.

DANGER!

Scientists discovered that some rain forest frogs release poisons through their skin to stop animals from eating them. These are also lethal to humans. An amount of poison the size of a grain of salt from the golden poison arrow frog can cause death.

Finding New Medicines

Some rain forest scientists research the chemicals in plants, especially the toxins or poisons, which might be useful in medicines. For example, a plant with bark which fungi do not grow on, and that insects do not eat, because of the *toxins* it contains, is used in medicine to treat *rheumatism*. About 1 percent of all plants have been screened for useful chemicals for medicines, yet one-quarter of all drugs are derived from rain forest ingredients, including two anti-*cancer* drugs from the poisonous rosy periwinkle plant of Madagascar (see page 24).

▼ Many medicines are made from or inspired by substances found in rain forest plant, animal and insect species. When these medicines are taken by or injected into patients, they can save lives.

GLOBAL AIR CONDITIONER

Researchers have discovered that rain forests help control gases, temperature, and water levels in the *atmosphere* around Earth. They are rather like a global air-conditioning system!

Gas Exchange

Trees take in *carbon dioxide* and water, and release oxygen in the process of *photosynthesis*. Using gas sensors on individual leaves, scientists have estimated that the Amazon rain forest alone stores 100 to 157 billion tons (90 to 140 billion t) of carbon, mostly as wood, and releases 20 percent of the world's *oxygen*. Deforestation reduces the oxygen supply because there are fewer trees, and it also creates more carbon dioxide, for example when trees are burned to clear land. The extra carbon dioxide in the atmosphere, added to that which is released by burning fossil fuels to power machines, is thought to cause *global warming*.

The water rain forests produce and hold is vital for rain forest wildlife.

Rain Forests and Water

Researchers have discovered that a rain forest creates up to 75 percent of its own rainfall in a closed system. Water in canopy leaves *evaporates* fast in high rain forest temperatures. This water vapor *condenses* on *bacteria* in the atmosphere above, forming clouds. Rain falls from the clouds back down into forest soil, rivers, and streams. However, this system is being broken down by deforestation. Fewer trees means less rainfall, so streams dry up, plants die, and soil (no longer bound by plant roots) is blown or washed away by storms.

Lush rain forest vegetation benefits from the constant supply of water in the rain forest's unique water system.

Rain forests are named for the rain clouds they create above them.

CUTTING EDGE

Some rain forest researchers use networks of sensors on cables strung between towers to automatically monitor temperature, humidity, rainfall, and carbon dioxide levels. Data from the sensors reveals the interaction between the forest and atmosphere in more detail than from a single monitoring point.

BILLION-DOLLAR FOREST

Drug companies can make huge profits from selling medicines they produce from rain forest species.

It costs a great deal of money to build and run rain forest labs and to pay for research equipment and scientists' salaries. Hundreds of governments, companies, and charities spend billions of dollars each year on rain forest research.

Bio-Prospecting

Drug companies and medical charities fund research into new active ingredients for medicines. This is called "bioprospecting." They do this partly because they can sell the medicines for a lot of money. For example, the drug company Eli Lilly earned around US$100 million each year for decades from sales of its anti-cancer drugs derived from the rain forest rosy periwinkle. Using these anti-cancer drugs has increased the survival of children with leukemia from 20 to 80 percent.

Local people, such as this boy from Equatorial Guinea, can benefit from the money large companies pay to research the rain forest.

Owning Forest

Some drug companies pay bio-prospecting fees to governments or organizations in the countries in which they research. For example, in 1992, drug company Merck paid a Costa Rican research center more than $1 million to supply plants and insects for its drug-screening programs. Merck also agreed to pay a percentage of profits on any drug sales resulting from Costa Rican organisms. When a company has designed a new medicine, it applies for a *patent*. This gives the company exclusive use of its invention, which can earn the company millions of dollars.

Drugs discovered in rain forests are developed in labs in other countries and then manufactured in different places.

CUTTING EDGE

In 2009, researchers at the Carnegie Institution for Science developed a system of sensors and small airplanes to create 3-D maps of the chemicals in rain forest plants. Spotting the promise of the system, the Gordon and Betty Moore Foundation awarded the researchers more than US$5 million to improve the technology so it is possible to identify plants by their chemical "fingerprint."

SHARING SCIENCE

After scientists have collected and studied data and compiled the results of their research, they share those findings with fellow scientists, governments, and other organizations to make a difference to people's lives.

Acting on Results

After scientists have collected and studied data, they write up their findings in journals or present them at conferences to share and compare them with discoveries made by other scientists. Then they pass on findings to newspapers and other *media*, governments, and charities so that the facts can be used to bring about change. For example, after researchers revealed the dangers of deforestation in the 1980s, the Forest Stewardship Council (FSC) was set up in 1993. This international, non-profit organization checks that trees are being cut legally and in a way that does not damage the forests, the people who live in them, and the environment.

When people buy wood products, such as paper, marked with this FSC logo, they know that buying them will not mean harming the world's forests.

These Earth scientists are sharing the valuable information that each one has discovered in his or her special area.

26

A scientist may work alone in his or her lab, but sharing research is vital.

Plant to Medicine

When scientists discover plants that could be used for medicines, they either share their discoveries or work with other scientists testing those chemicals in laboratories. They have to test doses required, how well they work, and if they cause side effects. They may do this by testing the drugs on *micro-organisms*, animals, or human volunteers. This process can take 10 to 15 years before the medicines are licensed for sale. It is a long process involving many scientists and there are many failures: on average, only 250 out of 20,000 plants tested prove useful.

CUTTING EDGE

Researchers are testing lesser-known species of tree to see how hard-wearing they are. These can be sold to building companies and manufacturers instead of them using the precious rain forest trees that are becoming more rare.

SECRETS OF THE RAIN FOREST

Researchers have already discovered some of the secrets of the rain forests and if they get the chance, they are likely to discover many more. Some of these discoveries, such as new medicines, directly benefit humankind. Others enrich people's lives.

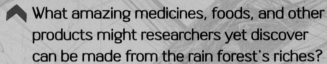

⌃ What amazing medicines, foods, and other products might researchers yet discover can be made from the rain forest's riches?

⌃ Orangutans spend about 90 percent of their lives in trees, but because of hunting and logging, these apes are now in danger of extinction.

Saving Our Future

Scientists have shown that forests currently absorb around 10 percent of the world's carbon dioxide *emissions*. Perhaps the most important research scientists are doing into rain forests today is what will happen if too many trees are cut and burned down. Many believe that if forests die and are replaced by bushes and shrubs that do not create their own rainfall system, these plants will dry out in the heat and be prone to fire. If this happens, rain forest regions will stop halting global warming and could even accelerate it.

Saving People, Saving Rain Forests

There are still many species of plants yet to be discovered and researched in the rain forest, some of which could be vital in fighting disease. This means that rain forest land has much more economic value today, and more potential than timber and farmland to make money in the future. With this information, governments might sign up to protecting rain forests in the future.

▼ Researchers are trying to find ways to balance the demands of business, such as farming, with the needs of the rain forest.

CUTTING EDGE

Some researchers are studying how fungi that grows on rubber trees in the Amazon rain forest produces chemicals that break down plastics. They believe this could be part of the solution to the worldwide problem of plastic waste.

GLOSSARY

atmosphere The layer of gases surrounding Earth.

bacteria A single-celled, microscopic, plant-like organism.

biodiversity The variety of plant and animal life in a particular habitat or ecosystem.

caimans Small freshwater alligators.

cancer A disease caused by an uncontrolled spread of abnormal cells in the body.

canopy The top layer of trees and branches in a forest.

carbon dioxide A gas in the atmosphere that is linked to global warming.

climate The usual pattern of weather that happens in a place.

condenses Changes from a gas into liquid (such as water vapor to water).

conservation The protection of something endangered such as rain forest.

data Information such as facts and statistics.

deforestation Cutting or burning down large areas of trees.

droppings Animal poop.

ecosystem A community of plants and animals and their physical surroundings.

emissions Gases released into the atmosphere.

evaporates Changes from a liquid into a gas (such as water to water vapor).

fungi A living thing that grows on other plants or rotting matter.

global warming Changes in the Earth's weather patterns caused by human activity.

GPS (Global Positioning System) A system that uses signals from satellites in space to locate positions on Earth.

humidity The amount of water vapor in the air.

infrared A type of light that is invisible.

media Newspapers, television, Internet, and other ways in which information is relayed to the public.

micro-organisms Microscopic living things.

organism A living thing.

oxygen A gas in the atmosphere that living things need to breathe.

patent A license that gives a company or individual the exclusive rights to an invention for a set period of time.

photosynthesis The process by which plants make food from carbon dioxide and water using energy from sunlight.

photovoltaic The process that produces electricity from sunlight.

poaching The illegal killing of animals.

pollution When air, soil, or water are spoiled or made dirty or harmful by something else.

renewable Something that can be replaced.

rheumatism A painful disorder of the joints or muscles.

satellites Manmade pieces of equipment that orbit Earth.

sensors Devices that detect and measure things, such as amounts of a particular gas in the air.

species A particular type of plant or animal.

toxins Poisons made by animals or plants.

water vapor When water is a gas in the air. Water comes in three states: liquid, gas (vapor), and solid (ice).

FURTHER READING

Books

Amazing Animal Adaptions: Rainforest Animal Adaptations. Lisa Amstutz, Capstone Press, 2012.

Discover More: Rainforest. Penny Arlon, Scholastic, 2013.

Explorer Travel Guides: Rainforests. Nick Hunter, Raintree, 2013.

Mapping Global Issues: Rainforest Destruction. Peter Littlewood, Smart Apple Media, 2012.

Unstable Earth: What Happens If the Rainforests Disappear? Mary Colson, Wayland, 2013.

Websites

Read about a day in the life of a rain forest scientist at:
www.nasa.gov/centers/ames/research/factsheets/FS-021101ARC.html

Find out where rain forests of the world are at:
www.srl.caltech.edu/personnel/krubal/rainforest/Edit560s6/www/where.html

Read news and facts and watch videos about rain forests at:
www.bbc.co.uk/nature/habitats/Tropical__and__subtropical__moist__broadleaf__forests

Watch a short video about how and why the FSC was set up at:
www.fsc-uk.org/our-history.26.htm

INDEX